dabblelab

AMAZING MAGIC TRICKS
HOCUS POCUS!
TRICKS FOR AMATEUR MAGICIANS

4D™
A MAGICAL AUGMENTED READING EXPERIENCE

• • • BY NORM BARNHART • • •

CAPSTONE PRESS
a capstone imprint

Dabble Lab is published by
Capstone Press, A Capstone Imprint
1710 Roe Crest Drive
North Mankato, Minnesota 56003
www.mycapstone.com

Library of Congress Cataloging-in-Publication Data
Names: Barnhart, Norm, author.
Title: Hocus pocus! : tricks for amateur magicians : 4D a magical augmented reading experience / by Norm Barnhart.
Description: Mankato, Minn. : Capstone Press, 2018. | Series: Dabble lab. Amazing magic tricks 4D |
  Includes bibliographical references and index. | Audience: Age 8-12. | Audience: Grade 4 to 6.
Identifiers: LCCN 2017035463 (print) | LCCN 2017039149 (ebook) | ISBN 9781543505740 (eBook PDF) |
  ISBN 9781543505696 (library binding)
Subjects: LCSH: Magic tricks—Juvenile literature.
Classification: LCC GV1548 (ebook) | LCC GV1548 .B3636 2018 (print) | DDC 793.8—dc23
LC record available at https://lccn.loc.gov/2017035463

• • • • • •

EDITOR:
Aaron J. Sautter

DESIGNER:
Ted Williams

PRODUCTION:
Katy LaVigne

• • • • • •

Image Credits
All photographs and video are done by Capstone Studio

Design Elements
Shutterstock: findracadabra, G.roman, javarman, popular business

Printed and bound in the USA.
010758S18

TABLE OF CONTENTS

✪ MYSTERIOUS MAGIC! 4

✪ THE MAGIC ROBOT 6

✪ AMAZING SPORTS PREDICTION 8

✪ THE PHOENIX BALLOON.................. 10

✪ THE AMAZING BRAIN-E-O 12

✪ THE PUZZLING PUZZLE.................. 14

✪ IT'S PARTY TIME! 18

✪ THE FREAKY MIND WELD................. 20

✪ MESSAGE FROM A GHOST 22

✪ WHERE'S ROVER?..................... 24

✪ RICKY, THE WONDER RABBIT 26

GLOSSARY............................ 30

READ MORE 31

INTERNET SITES 31

INDEX 32

MYSTERIOUS MAGIC!

Magicians have performed mysterious magic tricks for hundreds of years. They have rarely shared their secrets with anyone. But by opening this book, you'll learn to make things vanish or appear, and you'll astound audiences with mysterious mental powers. It's time to do some magic!

THE KEYS TO MAGIC

✪ **Practice, practice, practice!** Try standing in front of a mirror while practicing with your props. Then you can see what the tricks look like to your audience.

✪ **Keep it secret!** If you reveal the secrets of a trick, people won't be very impressed. It also ruins the trick for other magicians.

✪ **Be entertaining!** Tell the audience jokes or stories while you do your tricks. It will keep them coming back for more.

A MAGIC SECRET – SECRET ASSISTANTS

Magicians often have secret assistants who know how the tricks work. Sometimes they sit in the crowd and pretend to be part of the audience. Secret assistants help the magician make the tricks look real. Find a good secret assistant and you'll have lots of fun fooling people with your magic tricks.

DOWNLOAD THE CAPSTONE 4D APP!

- Ask an adult to search in the Apple App Store or Google Play for "Capstone 4D".
- Click Install (Android) or Get, then Install (Apple).
- Open the app.
- Scan any of the following spreads with this icon:

When you scan a spread, you'll find fun extra stuff to go with this book! You can also find these things on the web at **www.capstone4D.com** using the password **magic.amateur**

MEET THE MAGICIAN! ⭐

Norm Barnhart is a professional comic magician who has entertained audiences for nearly 40 years. In 2007 Norm was named America's Funniest Magician by the Family Entertainers Workshop. Norm's travels have taken him across the United States and to many countries around the world. He also loves to get kids excited about reading. Norm says, **"I love to bring smiles to people of all ages with magic. After reading this book, kids will love performing magic tricks for their friends too."**

THE MAGIC ROBOT

These robots seem to have magical abilities! In this trick, the audience will gasp when they see a toy robot magically transport from your pocket back to its box.

WHAT YOU NEED

★ Two identical toy robots
★ A small box
★ Scissors

PREPARATION

1. First, cut a hole in the side of the box as shown. The hole should only be large enough to fit your finger. Then place both robots into the box.

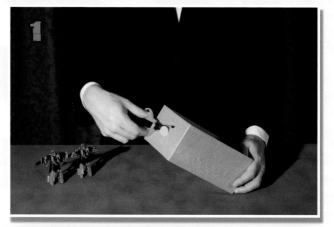

PERFORMANCE

1. Start by picking up the box with one finger inside the hole. Hold one toy robot with your finger as shown. Next, tip over the box to drop the second robot into your open hand. Be sure to tip the box toward yourself so the audience won't see the secret robot inside.

MAGIC TIP Be sure to keep the hole in the box hidden at all times. If the audience sees it, they'll learn the secret of the trick.

2. Next, hold up the robot and show it to the audience. Tell them a story about how it can perform an amazing magic act. Explain how it can move so fast that they won't even see it move. Then place the robot in your pocket.

3. Hold up the box and wave your magic wand over it. You can say some made-up magic words to help fool the audience. Or you can pretend that you feel something jump out of your pocket and into the box.

4. Finally tip over the box to drop the secret robot into your hand. Show it to the audience and have it take a bow!

SEE HOW IT'S DONE

AMAZING SPORTS PREDICTION

Do you like sports? Trying to guess the winner of a game is almost impossible. But with this trick, you'll amaze everyone when you predict each ball before it's pulled from the bag.

WHAT YOU NEED

- ✪ Several small toy sports balls
- ✪ A small paper bag
- ✪ Scissors

PREPARATION

1. First, cut a small secret hole in the bottom back corner of the paper bag as shown.

2. Then fold the bag back again so the hole is hidden.

SEE HOW IT'S DONE

1. First, tell the audience about your amazing predictions. Tell them you can guess which ball will be pulled out of the bag.

Pick up the bag and unfold it, making sure to keep the hole hidden. Pinch the hole closed so nobody sees it, then show the audience that the bag is empty.

2. Now, ask a volunteer to drop the balls into the bag. Be sure to hold the bag so the secret hole faces you. You should be able to see a bit of one ball through the secret hole. If you see the baseball say, "I predict that the baseball will be picked first."

3. Finally, reach into the back corner of the bag and quickly pull out the baseball. Show it to the audience to prove you predicted the correct ball. Return the balls to the bag and repeat the trick two more times, announcing which ball will be picked each time. Finally, crumple up the bag and toss it in your magic trunk. Everyone will wonder how you made your amazing predictions!

THE PHOENIX BALLOON

Is it possible to put a popped balloon back together again? It is with this fun trick! The audience will be stunned when they see a popped balloon magically made whole again.

WHAT YOU NEED

★ Two identical balloons
★ A large paper bag
★ A fork

PREPARATION

1. First, blow up one balloon and tie it. Then place it at the bottom of the paper bag as shown. Place the empty balloon in the bag so it can be dumped out easily.

PERFORMANCE

1. Start by telling the audience about your magic balloon. Say, "This balloon can restore itself if it's popped!" Then tip over the bag so the empty balloon drops onto the table. Don't let the secret filled balloon fall out.

MAGIC TIP

Try adding some fun to this trick. Pretend that the balloon pieces are jumping around in the bag as they try to join together again.

2. Next, blow up the empty balloon, tie it, and show it to the audience. Then pop it with the fork and place the pieces back into the bag. You can have fun by saying something like, "This looks bad. I don't know if the balloon can fix itself this time!"

3. Now, close the top of the bag and wave your magic wand over it. You can say a few made-up magic words too.

4. Finally, open up the bag and pull out the secret filled balloon. The audience will think the popped balloon magically restored itself. Take a bow as they applaud!

SEE HOW IT'S DONE

THE AMAZING BRAIN-E-O

Use the power of your brain to read people's minds! Your friends will be amazed as you tell them what objects they are thinking about. It's easy when you know the secret.

PERFORMANCE

1. Start this trick by talking about your amazing mind-reading powers. Tell the audience that you can read their minds — and you can prove it. Have your secret assistant sit with the audience. When you peform this trick, ask him or her to come up and help you.

2. Then turn your back to the audience. While your back is turned, your assistant asks someone in the audience to choose a prop on the table. The volunteer should not say the object's name out loud. Instead, the volunteer should just point at the chosen object.

MAGIC TIP

Try this trick a second time, but next time the chosen prop will be the sixth one the assistant points to. The audience will wonder how you can read their minds!

3. Before doing this trick, you should arrange to have your assistant point at the chosen prop on the third try. Now, turn back to the table. Your assistant should point to a different object and ask if it is the chosen item. You'll say, "No, that's not correct."

4. Your assistant then points to a second item on the table. Concentrate hard on that object and act as if you aren't sure if it's correct. Finally, you'll say, "No that's not the right one either."

5. On the third try, your assistant will point at the correct object. Now, act like the trick has become really easy and say, "Yes, that's it!" The audience will be stunned by your amazing mind-reading powers!

SEE HOW IT'S DONE

THE PUZZLING PUZZLE

You can use your mental powers to do more than just guess what people are thinking. You will really leave your audience puzzled with this mind-bending puzzle trick!

WHAT YOU NEED

⭐ Two identical puzzles   ⭐ Scissors
⭐ Two paper bags   ⭐ Tape

PREPARATION

1. First, cut one bag in half lengthwise as shown. Be sure to leave the bottom of the bag attached.

2. Then place the cut bag inside the whole bag. Tape the sides to hold it in place. This creates a secret pocket on one side where you can hide a puzzle.

3. Next, assemble one of the puzzles, but leave one piece out. Then slide the puzzle into the secret pocket.

1. First, tell the audience about your mysterious mind powers. Say, "Puzzles are fun, but they take too long to put together. I like using magic instead." Then tip the bag over to show the audience that it's empty. As you tip it, hold the secret pocket closed to hide the puzzle.

MAGIC TIP Use some glue or tape on the back of the hidden puzzle to hold it together while it's inside the bag.

2. Next, take out the second identical puzzle. Drop the loose pieces into the bag, leaving one piece on the table. This piece should match the one you left out earlier. You can mark the back of it to remember which piece it is.

3. Now, shake the bag gently and wave your magic wand over it. Or pretend that you're concentrating hard to put the puzzle together with the power of your mind.

4. Slide the hidden puzzle out of the bag. Be sure the audience can see that the puzzle is fully assembled, except for one missing piece. Then toss the bag into your magic trunk.

5. Finally, place the extra puzzle piece into the puzzle. Leaving one piece out helps the audience believe that you really assembled the puzzle with magic. Take a bow while the audience applauds your mysterious mental powers!

SEE HOW IT'S DONE

IT'S PARTY TIME!

Celebrate the New Year, a friend's birthday, or any special occasion with this fun, flashy trick. You'll be the life of the party when you make a shower of confetti instantly appear.

WHAT YOU NEED
- ✪ Two identical file folders
- ✪ A sheet of colored paper
- ✪ A marker
- ✪ Scissors
- ✪ Glue

PREPARATION

1. First, cut 1 inch (2.5 centimeters) off the top of one folder. Then glue one side of the short folder inside the other folder as shown.

2. Next, cut the sheet of paper in half. Using the marker, write a message like "Happy New Year!" on both halves of the paper. Then cut one half of the paper into confetti. Place it in one of the open sections inside the folder as shown.

MAGIC TIP
Make sure none of the confetti falls out when you show the empty folder to the audience. If they see it, they'll know you cheated!

18

1. Tell the audience, "It's time for a party!" Then show them the empty section of the folder.

Next, show the audience the uncut paper with the message written on it. Then place it into the empty section of the folder.

2. Now it's time for the magic. Concentrate hard on the folder and say a few magic words. Pretend that you're cutting up the paper inside with magic invisible scissors.

3. Finally, pop open the folder so a shower of confetti fills the air! Be sure to keep the uncut paper hidden inside the closed section of the folder. Put the folder in your magic trunk and take a bow!

SEE HOW IT'S DONE

THE FREAKY MIND WELD

Paper clips are easy to lose. It's easier to keep track of them if they're linked together. This trick will astonish your audience when they see your magic mental powers at work!

WHAT YOU NEED

★ 20 paper clips
★ An envelope
★ Glue

PREPARATION

1. First, link together 10 paper clips and place them in the corner of the envelope. Next, glue the inside of the envelope as shown to make a secret pocket. The linked clips will be sealed inside. Then put the 10 loose clips into the open part of the envelope.

Glue here.

PERFORMANCE

1. Show the envelope to the audience and say, "I found an easy way to keep paper clips together." Open the envelope and pour out the loose clips.

MAGIC TIP

Try attaching a small toy soldier to the end of the paper clip chain. Then pretend to be surprised when you find that the soldier did all the work!

2. Tell the audience, "All I have to do is link the clips together with my mind." Put the clips back in the envelope, one at a time. Count out loud as you do this so the audience knows how many paper clips there are. Then lick the envelope and seal it.

3. Now, hold the envelope up to your forehead. Pretend to use your powerful mental energy to link the paper clips together. Pretending to concentrate hard makes this trick seem really mysterious for the audience.

4. Now, rip open the end of the envelope with the secret pocket. Grab the end of the linked clips and slowly pull them out. The audience will be astonished when they see that the clips are linked together. You have one powerful brain!

SEE HOW IT'S DONE

MESSAGE FROM A GHOST

You can freak out your friends with this spooky trick. When your pet ghost sends you a creepy message, they'll be too scared to move!

PREPARATION

1. Write a creepy message like "Boo!" on one sheet of paper. Crumple the message into a ball. Then place it into the shoebox with the blank sheet of paper. Place the marker in your pocket.

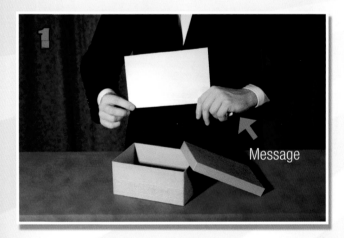

Message

PERFORMANCE

1. Tell your friends you have a pet ghost and that it likes to leave you messages. Get out the shoebox and take out the blank sheet of paper. At the same time, secretly hide the crumpled secret message in your hand as shown.

MAGIC TIP

Before doing this trick, try telling the audience a story about the ghost. Maybe you trapped it by the light of the full moon. Or maybe it's a friendly ghost that likes to help out with your magic show!

Message

Blank paper

2. Show the audience that the flat paper is blank on both sides, then crumple it into a ball. As you crumple it, secretly switch it with the secret message hidden in your hand. Then drop the secet message into the shoebox. Keep the crumpled blank paper hidden in your hand.

3. Next, get the marker from your pocket. As you do this, leave the crumpled blank paper behind in your pocket. Put the marker into the box and then put the cover on top. Begin shaking the box and pretending to wrestle with it as if your pet ghost is moving around inside.

4. Finally, remove the shoebox cover and take out the paper with the secret message. Ask someone to open it and read it. Your friends will be amazed at the spooky message that has appeared!

SEE HOW IT'S DONE

WHERE'S ROVER?

Mental magic can help you read people's minds, make predictions, or put a puzzle together. And with this astounding trick, it can even help you find a lost dog!

PERFORMANCE

1. First, show the toy dog and the cups to the audience, then set the props on the table. Tell the audience you have a special mental connection with the dog. Say, "Rover is my special pal. I can find him even if he gets lost under the cups."

2. Next, ask your secret assistant, who is sitting in the audience, to come and help you with this trick. Then turn your back to the table. Ask your secret assistant to place the toy dog under one of the cups and mix them up.

MAGIC TIP

Be sure to practice this trick with your secret assistant before performing it. If he or she acts cool and calm, everything should go smoothly.

3. Turn back to the table when your assistant is done. Then begin pretending to use your mental powers to see which cup the dog is under.

You will be able to find the correct cup by looking at your secret assistant's feet.

4. If the dog is under the left cup, your assistant's foot will point to the left.

If the dog is under the center cup, your assistant's feet both point forward.

If the dog is under the right cup, your assistant's foot will point to the right.

5. Once you know where the toy dog is, lift up the cup to reveal the toy. The audience will be stunned by your awesome mental powers!

SEE HOW IT'S DONE

RICKY, THE WONDER RABBIT

Magicians love using rabbits in their acts. But some rabbits are fun tricksters themselves! You can astonish your friends with this card trick using a tricky stuffed bunny.

WHAT YOU NEED

⭐ A deck of cards
⭐ A stuffed toy rabbit

PREPARATION

1. Place all the red cards on the bottom of the deck and all the black cards on the top. When fanned out, the black cards and red cards should be grouped together as shown.

PERFORMANCE

1. Start by introducing Ricky the Wonder Rabbit to your audience. Say, "Ricky can find a secret hidden card with his amazing sense of smell!"

2. Next, fan out the top half of the deck as shown. Make sure that only the black cards are fanned out. Then ask a volunteer to choose a card and show it to the audience, but not to you or Ricky the Rabbit. This should be one of the black cards.

3. While the volunteer shows the card to the audience, fan out the bottom half of the deck so only the red cards are fanned out. Ask the volunteer to slide the chosen card back into the fanned part of the deck.

4. Now the black card should be mixed in with the red cards and very easy to find. This is the secret of the trick.

5. Now, fan out the deck so only you can see the cards. Take the chosen black card from the deck and lay it face down on the table. Tell the volunteer, "I'm not sure, but I think your card could be this one." Be sure to remember where this card is on the table.

6. Take five more cards and lay them on the table in the same way. There will be a total of six cards on the table. Each time you pick a card, tell the volunteer you think it could be the chosen card, but you aren't sure. Be sure to remember where the correct card is.

MAGIC TIP
You can make this trick really fun by pretending to scold Ricky for fooling you with his trickery!

7. Now it's time for Ricky the Wonder Rabbit to do his famous trick. Have some fun by handling the rabbit like a puppet. Have Ricky sniff a card. He'll shake his head "no." Flip over the card to show it's not the volunteer's chosen card.

8. Keep playing with Ricky like he's real. Have Ricky sniff at each card and shake his head "no" until there are just two cards left. Make sure one of the leftover cards is the correct one.

9. Now say, "Okay Ricky, there are only two cards left. This is your last chance." Have Ricky sniff at the correct card. Ricky should go wild — bouncing and jumping around. Finally, he'll land on the correct card. Flip over the chosen card and show it to the audience. Have Ricky take a bow as they applaud!

SEE HOW IT'S DONE

GLOSSARY

applaud (uh-PLAWD)—to show that you like something, usually by clapping your hands

assemble (uh-SEM-buhl)—to put all the parts of something together

assistant (uh-SIS-tuhnt)—a person who helps someone else do a job or perform a task

audience (AW-dee-uhnss)—people who watch or listen to a play, movie, or show

concentrate (KAHN-suhn-trayt)—to focus your thoughts and attention on something

confetti (kuhn-FET-ee)—small pieces of colored paper that people throw at parties, parades, and other celebrations

mental power (MEN-tuhl POU-ur)—the ability to do something with the mind, such as finding hidden objects or reading others' thoughts

predict (pri-DIKT)—to say what you think will happen in the future

prop (PROP)—an item used by an actor or performer during a show

trunk (TRUHNGK)—a large case or box used for storage or for carrying items

volunteer (vol-uhn-TIHR)—someone who offers to help perform a task during a show

READ MORE

Barnhart, Norm. *Dazzling Card Tricks.*
Magic Manuals. North Mankato, Minn.:
Capstone Press, 2014.

Hildyard, Anne. *Children's Book of Magic.*
New York: DK Publishing, 2014.

Turnbull, Stephanie. *Easy Coin Tricks.* Beginner
Magic. Mankato, Minn.: Smart Apple Media, 2014.

. . . .

INTERNET SITES

Use FactHound to find Internet sites
related to this book.

Visit www.facthound.com

Just type in 9781543505696 and go.

 Check out projects, games and lots more at
www.capstonekids.com

INDEX

assistants, 4, 12–13,
    24–25

balloons, 10–11

cards, 26–29

ghosts, 22–23

magic trunks, 9, 17, 19
magic wands, 7, 11, 16
magic words, 7, 11, 19
mental powers, 4, 12–13,
    14–17, 20–21, 24–25

parties, 18–19
practice, 4, 24
predictions, 8–9, 24
puzzles, 14–17

rabbits, 26–29

secrets, 4, 5, 6, 7, 8, 9, 10,
    11, 12, 14, 15, 20, 21,
    22, 23, 24, 25, 26, 27

toys, 6–7, 8–9, 20, 24–25,
    26–29

volunteers, 9, 12, 27–29